Englisch mit Elefant und Hase

At home

Berlin · Madrid · München · Warschau · Wien · Zürich

pillow

bed

curtains

soft toy

alarm clock

bedside table

bedroom

shower
bath
toilet paper
towel
toilet
sink

bathroom

fridge

microwave

kettle

oven

toaster

kitchen cupboard

kitchen

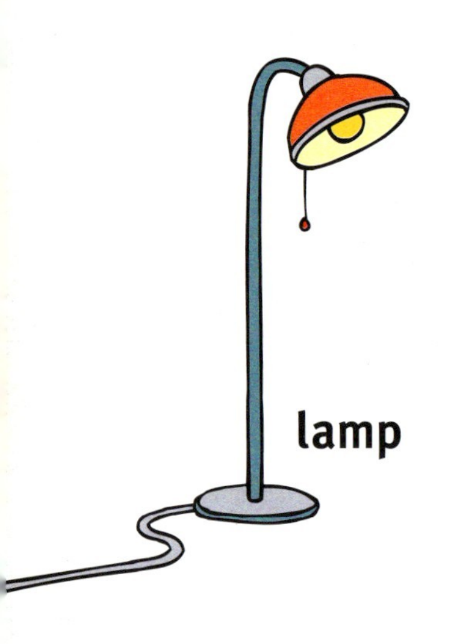

lamp

sofa

sofa cushion

armchair

coffee table

shelves

blanket

television

living room

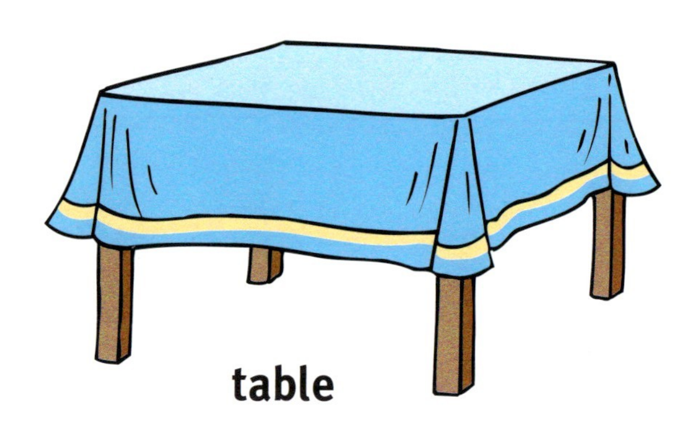

table

chair

place mats

vase

clock

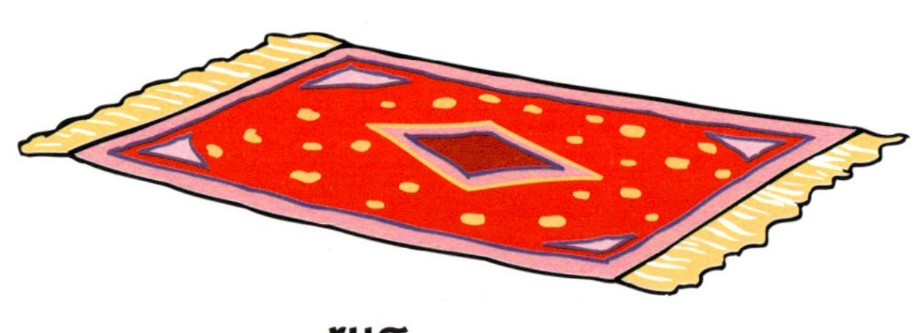

rug

dining room

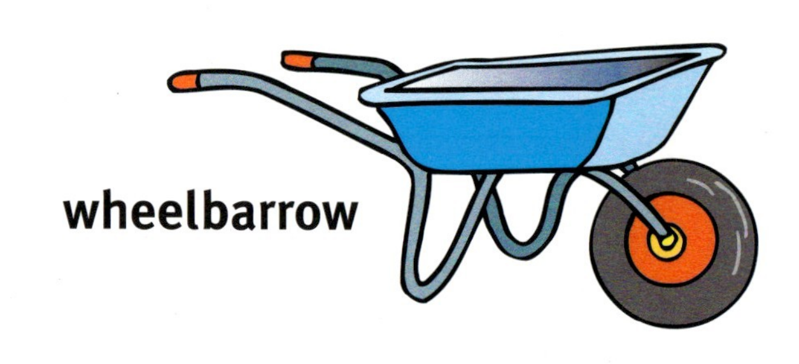

wheelbarrow

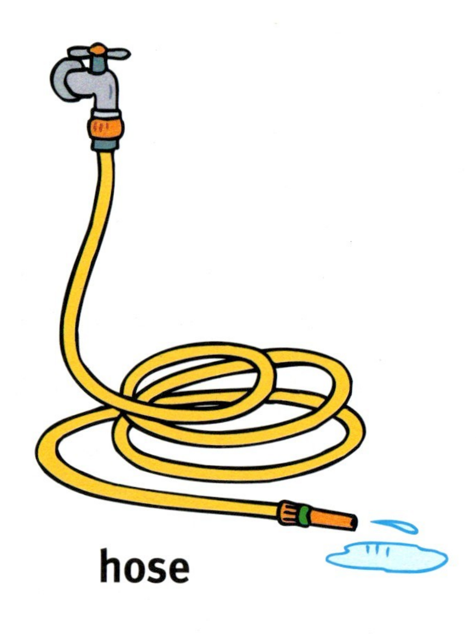

hose

watering can

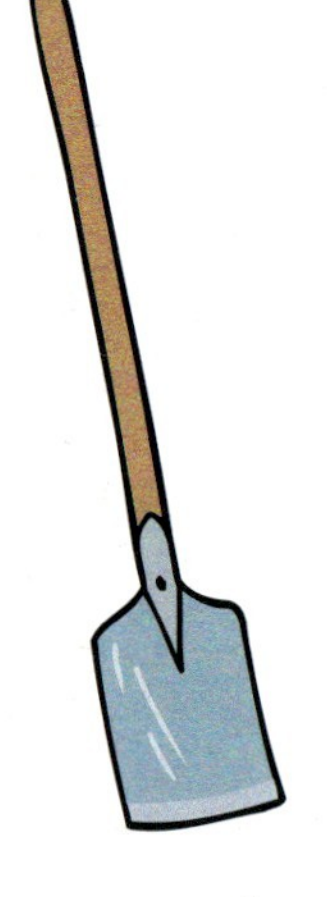

rubber boots

ladder

garden

washing powder

clothes line

pegs

washing machine

dryer

laundry room

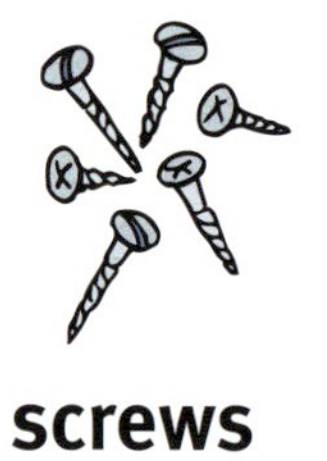

screws

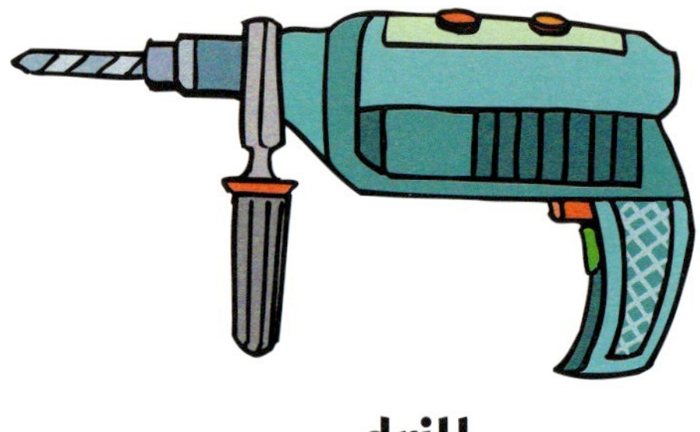

drill

screwdriver

pliers

hammer

nails

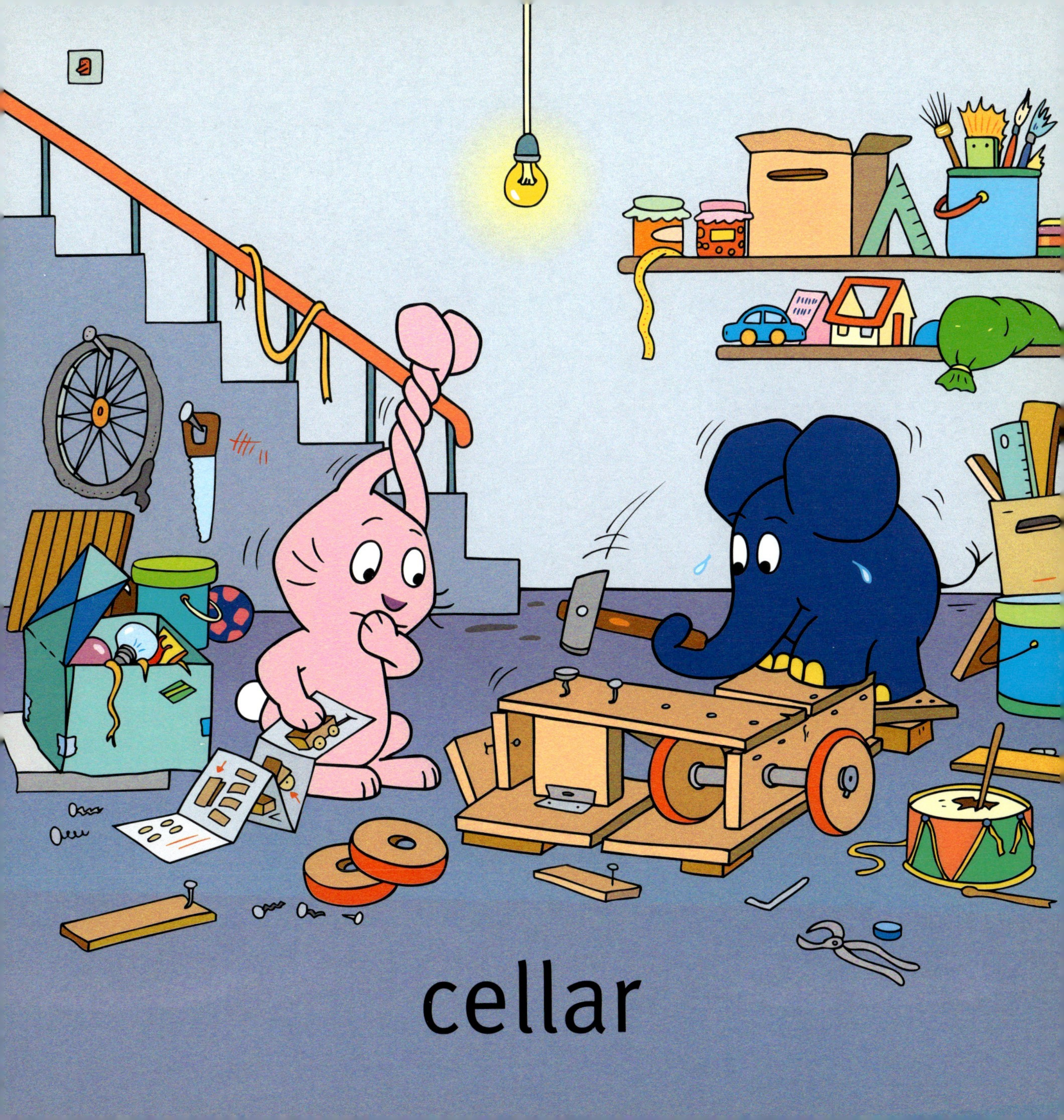

cellar

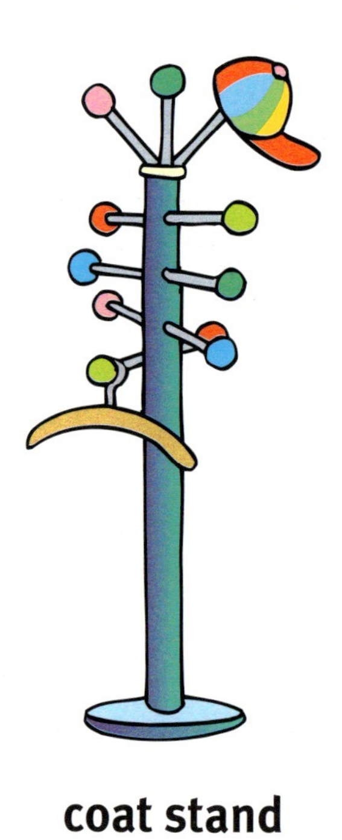

coat stand

sideboard

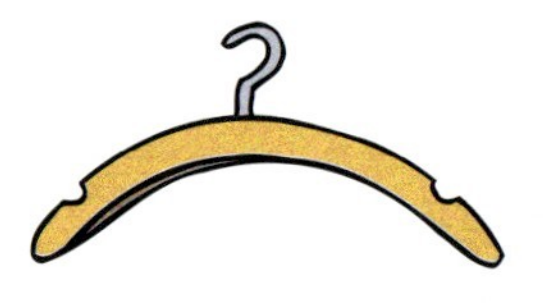

clothes hanger

keys

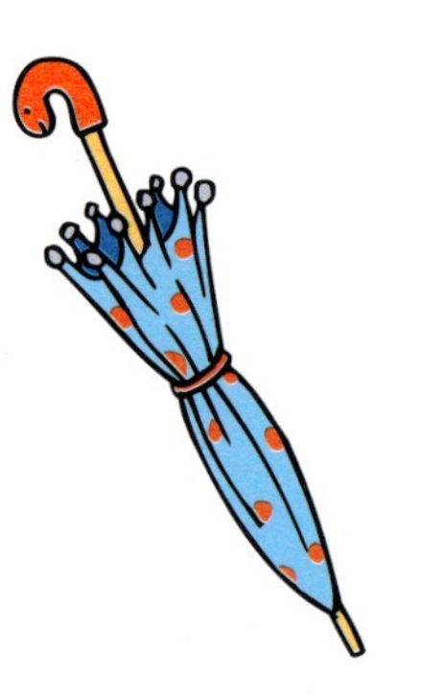

umbrella

shoes

hall

toy car

tricycle

tractor

scooter

bike

garage

wardrobe

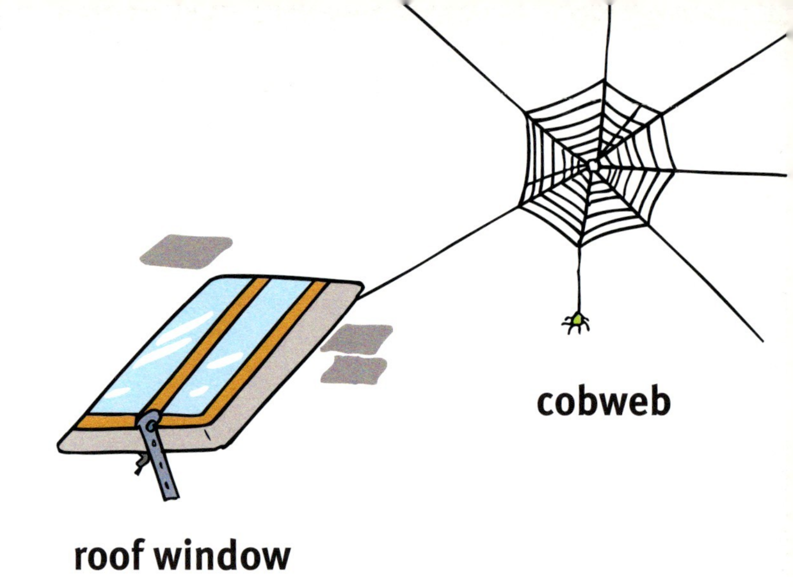

attic

Wörterliste

the alarm clock	ðɪ əˈlɑːm klɒk	der Wecker
the armchair	ðɪ ˈɑːmtʃeə	der Sessel
the attic	ðɪ ˈætɪk	der Dachboden
the bath	ðə ˈbɑːθ	die Badewanne
the bathroom	ðə ˈbɑːθruːm	das Badezimmer
the bed	ðə ˈbed	das Bett
the bedroom	ðə ˈbedruːm	das Schlafzimmer
the bedside table	ðə ˈbedsaɪd ˌteɪbl	der Nachttisch
the bike	ðə ˈbaɪk	das Fahrrad
the blanket	ðə ˈblæŋkɪt	die Decke
the box	ðə ˈbɒks	die Kiste
the cellar	ðə ˈselə	der Keller
the chair	ðə ˈtʃeə	der Stuhl
the clock	ðə ˈklɒk	die Uhr
the clothes hanger	ðə ˈkləʊðz ˌhæŋə	der Kleiderbügel
the clothes line	ðə ˈkləʊðz laɪn	die Wäscheleine
the coat stand	ðə ˈkəʊt stænd	der Kleiderständer
the cobweb	ðə ˈkɒbweb	die Spinnwebe
the coffee table	ðə ˈkɒfɪ ˌteɪbl	der Couchtisch
the curtains	ðə ˈkɜːtnz	die Vorhänge
the dining room	ðə ˈdaɪnɪŋ ˌruːm	das Esszimmer
the drill	ðə ˈdrɪl	die Bohrmaschine
the dryer	ðə ˈdreɪə	der Trockner
the fridge	ðə ˈfrɪdʒ	der Kühlschrank
the garage	ðə ˈgærɑːʒ	die Garage
the garden	ðə ˈgɑːdn	der Garten
the hall	ðə ˈhɔːl	die Diele
the hammer	ðə ˈhæmə	der Hammer
the hose	ðə ˈhəʊz	der Schlauch
the kettle	ðə ˈketl	der Wasserkocher
the keys	ðə ˈkiːz	die Schlüssel
the kitchen	ðə ˈkɪtʃən	die Küche
the kitchen cupboard	ðə ˈkɪtʃən ˌkʌbəd	der Küchenschrank
the ladder	ðə ˈlædə	die Leiter
the lamp	ðə ˈlæmp	die Lampe
the laundry room	ðə ˈlɔːndrɪ ˌruːm	die Waschküche